*f*P

Jeff Koon

Andy Powell

Illustrated by

Ward Schumaker

THE FREE PRESS
New York London Toronto Sydney Singapore

You May *Not* Tie an Alligator to a Fire Hydrant

101 Real Dumb Laws

THE FREE PRESS
A Division of Simon & Schuster, Inc.
1230 Avenue of the Americas
New York, NY 10020

Copyright © 2002 by Jeff Koon and Andy Powell
Illustrations copyright © 2002 by Ward Schumaker
All rights reserved, including the right of reproduction in
whole or in part in any form.

THE FREE PRESS and colophon are trademarks
of Simon & Schuster, Inc.

For information regarding special discounts for bulk purchases,
please contact Simon & Schuster Special Sales
at 1-800-456-6798 or business@simonandschuster.com

Designed by Bonni Leon-Berman

Manufactured in the United States of America

10 9   8   7   6   5

Library of Congress Cataloging-in-Publication Data

Koon, Jeff.
    You may not tie an alligator to a fire hydrant : 101 real
dumb laws / Jeff Koon, Andy Powell ; illustrated by Ward
Schumaker.
        p.   cm.
1. Law—United States—Humor.   I. Powell, Andy.
II. Schumaker, Ward.   III. Title.

K184.K66 2002
349.73'02'07—dc21   2002022059

ISBN 0-7432-3065-5

Contents

Preface

One of our founding fathers, Benjamin Franklin, told us that only two things in life are certain: death and taxes. Obviously, he didn't realize that there would always be laws to govern those certainties, as well as everything else in life. Laws have kept our nation from falling into chaos since Franklin's time; they were even pillars of civilization in the ancient world. However, once in a while we need to ask a question like: Does West Virginia really need a law telling children not to attend school with breath smelling of "wild onions?" Jeff and I are fans of fresh breath just as much as the next guy, but we doubt it's truly worthy of an act of Congress.

While the United States may be the most prolific producer of dumb laws, other nations have collections of their own. We've had a mere two hundred years or so to amass our collection, but countries such as the United Kingdom have been doing it since the Dark

Ages. Some countries have been dramatically accelerating their rate of collection lately too. According to a report on AP Worldstream in 1997, the Taliban regime in Afghanistan decreed that paper bags could not be used because there was a chance that the recycled paper they were made from might include recycled pages of the Koran. Laws from over two dozen countries make up the codex of dumb laws on our website.

Not all dumb laws started out as such. To be fair, there are some very sensible reasons for the existence of some of the laws listed in these pages. As a whole, they tend to fall into one of several categories.

Outdated laws

Once upon a time, long, long ago, many dumb laws had a real purpose, having been created to solve a problem that no longer exists. For example, in Florida it is illegal to block any traveled wagon roads. We don't think Florida's wagon roads are seeing much traffic these days, but we're sure it's best to keep them clear should someone decide to use them. Most outdated laws wouldn't survive if our lawmakers weren't so busy making new ones. We'd suggest that they do a little spring cleaning of the books, but then, what would my high school senior project be about?

Blue laws

These laws are designed to protect Sundays, our supposed day of rest. We're convinced that most Americans have privately outlawed rest in their lives, so maybe some mandatory rest isn't a bad idea. Blue laws range from the very general "No work may be done on Sundays" to the specific "You may not sell toothpaste and a toothbrush to the same customer on a Sunday."

Local laws

Many laws were created with a specific, reasonable purpose in mind, but when the law is taken out of its local context it seems ridiculous. In Pacific Grove, California, it is illegal to molest butterflies. The innuendo is mind-boggling. However, a little digging reveals that a certain butterfly is an endangered species and its entire population migrates through Pacific Grove. Sometimes laws aren't as dumb as they seem, but then, have you ever seen anyone molesting a butterfly?

Often people e-mail us after having visited the site and ask us about our "jobs". Several have asked me to represent them in court. Few people realize that we're high school seniors disguised as legal gurus by the thin veneer of the web. We have designed websites independently since the seventh grade, though we were met with little success. We met each other during the first week of our freshman year in high school, in a math class. Rather than pay attention to the lesson one day, we decided to start a website partnership with no idea what we were actually going to make a website about. We had formed our partnership with a single goal in mind, a somewhat typical goal for teenagers: to get as much attention as possible with no budget and only our spare time to work with. After several days spent searching for a topic, Jeff came up with the idea of putting together a collection of dumb laws. Dumb Laws, catchy name, right? However, in my infinite wisdom, I set up the site as "Stupid Laws," only because I forgot what we were really supposed to be named. Our site, "Stupid Laws," opened in October 1998. It was a fantastically amateur attempt at a website, but in 1998 it seemed as though everyone was starting a company, having an IPO, and making millions of dollars, so, like many other enterprising fourteen-year olds, we figured we'd jump in. We had no IPO and definitely didn't come close to making millions of dollars, but we stayed out of trouble. After Yahoo! spotted our site and made us one of 1998's Sites of the Year, we decided it was time to expand—and for a complete makeover. We changed our name back to "Dumb Laws" and set up shop at dumblaws.com. With our newfound publicity, a great web address, and a fresh design, the curtain rose on the second act of our careers.

Before long, thousands of people, then tens of thousands of people were browsing the information on our site daily. We frantically tried to keep pace with the new publicity, and enjoyed getting interviewed on radio and television. The site grew at an amazing pace, and money actually started rolling in. We bought new laptops and got more server space. And now we have a really cool book. We hope you enjoy it.

—*Andy Powell*

People

It is a felony to cut off your arm so as to make people feel sorry for you and give you money in Alabama.

Section 13A-14-1 Maiming one's self to escape duty or obtain alms

This law was created to keep people from injuring themselves in order to escape military service.

Every person who, with design to disable himself from performing a legal duty, existing or anticipated, shall inflict upon himself an injury whereby he is so disabled and every person who shall so injure himself with intent to avail himself of such injury to excite sympathy or to obtain alms or some charitable relief shall be guilty of a felony.

(Code 1923, §4941; Code 1940, T. 14, §357; Code 1975, §13-1-6.)

14

When skydiving at night in the United States, a person must wear a blinking beanie.

Section 105.33 Parachute jumps between sunset and sunrise

 (a) No person may make a parachute jump, and no pilot in command of an aircraft may allow any person to make a parachute jump from that aircraft, between sunset and sunrise, unless that person is equipped with a means of producing a light visible for at least 3 statute miles.

(Amdt. 105-7, 43 FR 22641, May 25, 1978)

In Utah first cousins can marry, but only after they are sixty-five years old.

Section 30-1-1 Incestuous marriages void

(2) First cousins may marry under the following circumstances:
　(a) both parties are 65 years of age or older; or
　(b) if both parties are 55 years of age or older, upon a finding by the district court, located in the district in which either party resides, that either party is unable to reproduce.

In Connecticut it is illegal for feeble-minded people to get married.

Okay,

they repealed

this one.

Now they can

get married.

Section 46-2 Marriage of imbeciles and feeble-minded persons prohibited

(General Statutes of Connecticut, Revised to 1997)

In Little Rock, Arkansas, it is illegal to honk your horn at a restaurant after dinner.

Section 18-54

 No person shall sound the horn on a vehicle at any place where cold drinks or sandwiches are served after 9:00 P.M.

In Kern County, California, it is illegal to play bingo while drunk.

Section 5.16.330 Intoxicated persons not to participate

No person who is in a state of intoxication shall be allowed to participate in a bingo game.

(Prior code §5480)

Perhaps California churches and nursing homes should simply stop serving alcohol.

In Alabama it is illegal to pretend to be a nun. No matter how good you might look.

Section 13A-14-4 Fraudulently pretending to be clergyman

Whoever, being in a public place, fraudulently pretends by garb or outward array to be a minister of any religion, or nun, priest, rabbi or other member of the clergy, is guilty of a misdemeanor and, upon conviction, shall be punished by a fine not exceeding $500.00 or confinement in the county jail for not more than one year, or by both such fine and imprisonment.

(Acts 1965, 1st Ex. Sess., No. 273, p. 381; Code 1975, §13-4-99.)

You may not *competitively* dance the night away in Alabama.

Section 13A-14-3 Marathon dance contests prohibited

(a) . . . it shall be unlawful for any person to participate in any marathon dance contest, walkathon contest or similar physical endurance contest by walking, dancing, riding or running continuing or intended to continue for a period of more than eight consecutive hours, whether or not an admission is charged or a prize awarded, and it shall be unlawful for any person to participate in more than one such contest or performance within any period of 48 hours.

In Delaware a person who wears a disguise during the commission of any felony is guilty of a felony. Got that?

Paragraph 1239 Wearing a disguise during the commission of a felony; class E felony

(a) A person who wears a hood, mask or other disguise during the commission of any felony is guilty of wearing a disguise during the commission of a felony. Wearing a disguise during the commission of a felony is a class E felony.

(b) A person may be found guilty of violating this section notwithstanding that the felony for which the person is convicted during which the person was wearing a disguise is a lesser included felony of the one originally charged.

Masked

evildoers

take

note.

In Connecticut no one may use a white cane unless they can't see it.

Critical information for the leisure-suit crowd: Next time you are accessorizing, avoid white canes.

Section 53-211 Use of white canes by others than blind persons prohibited

Vehicles to reduce speed, grant right-of-way.

(a) No person, except one wholly or partially blind, shall carry or use on any street or highway, or in any other public place, a cane or walking stick which is white in color or white tipped with red.

(b) Any driver of a vehicle who approaches or comes into the immediate vicinity of a person wholly or partially blind, carrying a white cane or a white cane tipped with red, or a person being guided by a guide dog, shall reduce speed or stop if necessary to grant the right-of-way to such person.

(c) Any person who violates any provision of this section shall be fined not more than one hundred dollars.

(1949 Rev., S. 8543; February, 1965, P.A. 448, S. 43.)

You may not pee in your back yard in San Luis Obispo, California, unless you have a good high fence.

Section 9.20.050 Urination in public

 No person shall urinate or defecate while on any city street, sidewalk, alley, roadway, parking lot, publicly maintained place or while in any other place, public or private, which is open to public view.

(Ord. 1083 §1, 1986)

In Belton, Missouri, it is illegal to have a snowball fight.

Section 15-20 Throwing missiles

No person shall throw any stone, snowball or any other missile upon or at any vehicle, building, tree or other public or private property, or upon or at any person in any public or private way or place or enclosed or unenclosed ground.

(Ord. No. 67-308, §6.12, 8-31-67)

30 minute sitcom

10 minute cigarette break

6 minute egg

5 minute ballot

In Arkansas no one may spend more than five minutes voting.

Section 7-5-309

(B) No voter shall be allowed more than five (5) minutes to mark his ballot.

After the era of the swinging chad, the dimpled chad, the hanging chad, and the pregnant chad, shouldn't we be giving people all the time they need to cast their ballot? Our grandparents take five minutes just to find their glasses.

It is illegal to have an illegal drink in Texas.

Section 103.01 Illicit Beverages Prohibited

No person may possess, manufacture, transport, or sell an illicit beverage.

(Acts 1977, 65th Leg., p. 505, ch. 194, §1, eff. Sept. 1, 1977.)

It is illegal to intentionally burp in church in Nevada.

Section (NRS) 201.270 Disturbing religious meetings

Every person who shall willfully disturb, interrupt or disquiet any assemblage or congregation of people met for religious worship:

1. By noisy, rude or indecent behavior, profane discourse, either within the place where such meeting is held, or so near it as to disturb the order and solemnity of the meeting;

2. By exhibiting shows or plays, or promoting any racing of animals, or gaming of any description, or engaging in any boisterous or noisy amusement;

3. By disturbing in any manner, without authority of law within 1 mile thereof, free passage along a highway to the place of such meeting, or by maliciously cutting or otherwise injuring or disturbing a conveyance or other property belonging to any person in attendance upon such meeting; or

4. By menacing, threatening or assaulting any person therein, shall be guilty of a misdemeanor.

(1911 C&P §213; RL §6478; NCL §10161] + [1911 C&P §332; RL §6597; NCL §10280)

In Daytona Beach, Florida, no one may swim in the ocean while tipsy.

Drown your sorrows elsewhere!

Section 10-56

It shall be unlawful for any person to swim or bathe in that portion of the Atlantic Ocean within the corporate limits of the city when under the influence of intoxicating liquor or narcotic drugs to the extent that his or her normal faculties are impaired.

(Code 1955, §28-64)

In South Carolina it is illegal to speak suggestively to your girlfriend.

Section 16-15-250 Communicating obscene messages to women

It is unlawful for a person to anonymously write, print, or by other manner or means, except by telephone, communicate, send, or deliver to another person within this State, any obscene, profane, indecent, vulgar, suggestive, or immoral message.

A person who violates the provisions of this section is guilty of a misdemeanor and, upon conviction, must be fined in the discretion of the court or imprisoned not more than three years, or both.

In Conyers, Georgia, no one may get the attention of any student in school without official permission.

Section 11-1-8 Schools, disturbing

 No person at or near any public school shall engage the attention of any pupil by conversation, sign or otherwise, to the disturbance of the school, nor shall any person carry away or remove from the school any pupil or attempt to remove or entice from the school any pupil without first securing the permission of school officials.

In Maui County, Hawaii, children must be twelve years old to play on a busy highway.

Section 9.20.020 Unlawful acts

It is unlawful for any child under the age of twelve years to play or loiter upon that portion of the public highway used for vehicular traffic in any congested district in the county as defined in this chapter; and any child so found loitering or playing upon such portion of the highway may be taken into custody by any police officer or the probation officer for the county and detained until the parent, guardian or person having custody, control, or supervision of the child calls for the child.

(Prior code §22-2.2)

You may beat up anyone who says really nasty things to you in Georgia.

Section 16-5-25 G

A person charged with the offense of simple assault or simple battery may introduce in evidence any opprobrious or abusive language used by the person against whom force was threatened or used; and the trier of facts may, in its discretion, find that the words used were justification for simple assault or simple battery.

Eavesdropping on your own conversation is a felony in Illinois.

No longer merely annoying, talking for the sake of hearing your own voice is now a felony. Maybe this isn't such a dumb law after all.

720 ILCS Section 5/14-2

You may be convicted of a Class 4 felony offense, punishable by up to three years in state prison, for the crime of "eavesdropping" on your own conversation.

In early May, all U.S. citizens should recognize the importance of the transportation system.

Title 36 Subtitle I Part A Chapter I Sec. 120. National Defense Transportation Day

The President is requested to issue each year a proclamation urging the people of the United States, including labor, management, users, and investors, in all communities served by the various forms of transportation to observe National Defense Transportation Day by appropriate ceremonies that will give complete recognition to the importance to each community and its people of the transportation system of the United States.

You may not sit on a street curb in Thousand Oaks, California.

Section 5-8.09 Prohibition on sitting and lying in certain public places

(c) Prohibitions. (1) No person shall sit or lie down upon a public sidewalk, street, curb, biking, walking or equestrian path, or in doorways and entrances to buildings; or upon a blanket, chair, stool, or any other object placed upon a public sidewalk, curb, biking, walking or equestrian path, or in doorways and entrances to buildings in any commercial zone (denoted with "C" on the City's Zoning Map).

(§ 1, Ord. 1300-NS, eff. October 23, 1997)

In Kentucky walking on the street in one's bathing suit was recently illegal. It was made legal again in 1974.

In the

Seventies

Kentucky

went wild.

Section 436.140

Any person who appears on any highway, or upon the street of any city that has no police protection, when clothed only in ordinary bathing garb, shall be fined no less than five dollars nor more than twenty-five dollars.

(KRS. Passed in 1922; Repealed in 1974)

44

In North Dakota no one can be arrested on the Fourth of July.

In addition to being Independence Day, the Fourth of July is now known in some circles as "Five Finger Discount Day."

Section 2331.12

No person shall be arrested during a sitting of the senate or house of representatives, within the hall where such session is being held, or in any court of justice, during the sitting of such court, or on Sunday, or on the fourth day of July.

In Indiana one can avoid paying for a dependent's medical care through prayer.

Section 5 (IC 35-46-1-5)

(a) A person who knowingly or intentionally fails to provide support to the person's dependent child commits nonsupport of a child, a Class D felony. However, the offense is a Class C felony if the amount of unpaid support that is due and owing is at least ten thousand dollars ($10,000).

(c) It is a defense that the accused person, in the legitimate practice of his religious belief, provided treatment by spiritual means through prayer, in lieu of medical care, to his dependent child.

If this can work for medical care, why can't it work for taxes?

(As added by Acts 1976, P.L. 148, SEC.6. Amended by Acts 1977, P.L. 340, SEC. 88; Acts 1978, P.L. 144, SEC. 9; P.L. 213-1996, SEC. 4)

In Massachusetts the Communist party is declared to be a subversive organization.

Chapter 264 Section 16A

The Communist Party is hereby declared to be a subversive organization.

Because the Communist party is a subversive organization, it is illegal.

Chapter 264 Section 17 Subversive organizations; prohibition

A subversive organization is hereby declared to be unlawful.

The state of Massachusetts has also decided to declare free speech illegal in a similar, one-law-in-two manner.

Anyone under eighteen playing pool in Kentucky must have a note from his or her mom or dad.

Section 436.320

No person owning or controlling a billiard or pool table shall permit, for compensation or reward, any minor under eighteen (18) years of age to play any game on the table, unless such minor shall have first displayed an identification card containing his name, age, photograph, and the signature of his parents or guardian. The minor shall keep such identification card on his person, and it shall be subject to inspection at any time by any peace officer. The person owning or controlling such billiard or pool table shall keep and maintain a registration book in which each minor shall sign. The person owning or controlling such billiard or pool table shall supply a blank identification card to each parent or guardian who makes request for same. Any person who violates this section shall be fined not less than ten ($10) nor more than one hundred dollars ($100) for each offense.

(KRS. Passed 1893; Amended in 1954, Ky. Acts ch. 232, sec. 1)

In Rhode Island it is illegal to challenge someone to a duel or to accept a duel, even if that duel is never fought.

Just think of the pay-per-view opportunities if dueling were permitted.

Paragraph 11-12-2 Challenging or accepting challenge to duel

Every person who shall challenge another to fight a duel with any dangerous weapon, to the hazard of life, and every person who shall accept a challenge to fight such duel, although no duel be fought, shall be imprisoned not exceeding seven years nor less than one year.

In West Lafayette, Indiana, people may not wander about in the street.

Section 45.04 Crossing roadways at right angles

No pedestrian shall cross a roadway except by a route at right angles to the curb or by the shortest route to the opposite curb except in a crosswalk.

(Code 1960, §16-71.)

In Wisconsin X-ray machines may not be used to fit shoes.

Section 941.34 Fluoroscopic shoe-fitting machines

Whoever uses, or possesses or controls with intent to so use, any fluoroscopic or X-ray machine for the purpose of shoe-fitting or attempting to fit shoes, or who knowingly permits such machine, whether in use or not, to remain on his or her premises, is subject to a Class B forfeiture.

(History: 1977 c. 173.)

In Galveston, Texas, playing frisbee on a beach is illegal.

Section 8-18. Playing ball, etc., on beach

It shall be unlawful for any person to engage in or play ball, frisbee or other games involving the use of a hard ball or other hard object upon a public beach, after being duly instructed and warned by the supervising lifeguard or police officer that any such game may not be played in the area under the circumstances prevailing at the time.

(Ord. No. 81-30, § 4, 4-2-81)

You may not lean over a bridge railing in Portland, Oregon.

16.70.240 Bridge Railings

No pedestrians may sit, stand on, or lean their torso over a Willamette River bridge railing unless engaged in bridge maintenance work or otherwise authorized by an appropriate government agency.

In Troutdale, Oregon, it is illegal to fight in a river.

Section 9.24.020 Unlawful acts in streams—General requirements

It is unlawful for any person to do any act while within a stream of water within the city which will endanger the life of any other person.

(Ord. 176 §2, 1972)

What is it about a stream that would make people think that endangering a life would be legal?

In Hillsboro, Oregon, no one may be towed behind a car on a skateboard.

Section 10.28.090 Clinging to other vehicles

No person riding upon any bicycle or skate-board shall attach it or himself or herself to any other vehicle upon a roadway.

(Prior code §7-3.9)

Let's admit it: At least once in our lives, car-skiing on a skateboard has sounded like a good idea. Or maybe it's just us.

In Tennessee children may not play games on Sunday without a license.

Paragraph 11-40-1 Work or recreation on Sunday prohibited

 Except as provided in §§5-22-6-5-22-11, inclusive, every person who shall do or exercise any labor or business or work of his or her ordinary calling, or use any game, sport, play, or recreation on the first day of the week, or suffer it to be done or used by his or her children, servants or apprentices, works of necessity and charity only excepted, shall be fined not exceeding five dollars ($5.00) for the first offense and ten dollars ($10.00) for the second and every subsequent offense; provided, further, however, that the above prohibitions shall not apply to any person or persons operating or functioning under a valid permit or license.

In Tennessee it is illegal for an atheist to hold a public office.

Article IX Disqualifications, Section 2. No atheist shall hold a civil office (Constitution of the State of Tennessee)

No person who denies the being of God, or a future state of rewards and punishments, shall hold any office in the civil department of this State.

It is illegal to spit on any sidewalk in Virginia.

Section 18.2-322 Expectorating in public places

 No person shall spit, expectorate, or deposit any sputum, saliva, mucus, or any form of saliva or sputum upon the floor, stairways, or upon any part of any public building or place where the public assemble, or upon the floor of any part of any public conveyance, or upon any sidewalk abutting on any public street, alley or lane of any town or city.

(Code 1950, §32-69; 1975, cc. 14, 15.)

In South Carolina every year before Halloween, all schoolchildren must be taught not to drink alcohol.

Section 53-3-20

The fourth Friday in October in each year shall be set apart and designated in the public schools as Francis Willard Day and in each public school it shall be the duty of such school to prepare and render a suitable program on the day to the end that the children of the State may be taught the evils of intemperance.

Animals

In Pacific Grove, California, it is illegal to molest butterflies.

Section 11.48.010

It is declared to be unlawful for any person to molest or interfere with, in any way, the peaceful occupancy of the monarch butterflies on their annual visit to the city of Pacific Grove, and during the entire time they remain within the corporate limits of the city, in whatever spot they may choose to stop in, provided, however, that if said butterflies should at any time swarm in, upon or near the private dwelling house or other buildings of a citizen of the city of Pacific Grove in such a way as to interfere with the occupancy and use of said dwelling and/or other buildings, that said butterflies may be removed, if possible, to another location upon the application of said citizen to the chief of police.

(Ord. 210 N.S. §8-3060, 1952)

When lepidopterans attack . . .

66

In Tuscaloosa, Alabama, it is illegal to get an animal drunk in a public park.

Section 18-24 Damage, etc., or injury to improvements, vegetation and wildlife

(9) Feeding of animals: To give or offer, or attempt to give, to any animal or bird, any tobacco, alcohol, or other poisonous or noxious substances.

(Code 1962, §24-33)

In Indiana it is illegal to color a bird.

Section 15-2.1-21-13(b)

A person who dyes, stains, or otherwise alters the natural coloring of a bird or rabbit commits a Class B misdemeanor.

(IC)

This law was enacted in order to keep people from coloring animals for sale, primarily around Easter.

In California pot-bellied pigs and lizards have the same rights as cats and dogs.

Food and Agricultural Code Section 31753

Any rabbit, guinea pig, hamster, pot-bellied pig, bird, lizard, snake, turtle, or tortoise legally allowed as personal property impounded in a public or private shelter shall be held for the same period of time, under the same requirements of care, and with the same opportunities for redemption and adoption by new owners or nonprofit, as defined in Section 501(c)(3) of the Internal Revenue Code, animal rescue or adoption organizations as cats and dogs. Section 17006 shall also apply to these animals. In addition to any required spay or neuter deposit, the pound or shelter, at its discretion, may assess a fee, not to exceed the standard adoption fee, for animals released to nonprofit animal rescue or adoption organizations pursuant to this section.

In Daytona Beach, Florida, you can't have too much undergrowth in your backyard.

Section 18-2 Weeds, trash, etc., as a public nuisance; removal by property owner or by city at owner's expense

(a) The existence of weeds, trash, undergrowth, brush, filth, garbage or other refuse on any lot, tract or parcel of land within the city which has caused the property to become, or which may reasonably cause the property to become infested, or inhabited by rodents, vermin or wild animals, or may furnish a breeding place for mosquitoes or threatens the public health, safety or welfare, or may reasonably cause disease or adversely affects and impairs the economic welfare of the adjacent property, is declared to constitute a public nuisance and is hereby prohibited.

Training a bear to wrestle is a felony in Alabama, and you lose the bear.

Section 13A-12-5 Unlawful bear exploitation; penalties

(a) A person commits the offense of unlawful bear exploitation if he or she knowingly does any one of the following:

(3) Sells, purchases, possesses, or trains a bear for bear wrestling.

(c) Upon the arrest of any person for violating this section, the arresting law enforcement officer, conservation officer, or animal control officer shall have authority to seize and take custody of any bear in the possession of the arrested person.

(Acts 1996, No. 96-468, p. 581, §1)

Perhaps as a punishment, those who subject bears to wrestling should have to wrestle their own bear. This would go well on pay-per-view along with the Rhode Island dueling.

In California it is illegal to own a snail, elephant, or sloth as a household pet. Pigs are okay.

Section 2118

It is unlawful to import, transport, possess, or release alive into this state, except under a revocable, nontransferable permit as provided in this chapter and the regulations pertaining thereto, any wild animal of the

following species:

(a) Class Aves: (birds)

The following species:

(b) Class Mammalia (mammals)

Order Edentata (sloths, anteaters, armadillos, etc.):

All species.

Order Proboscidea (elephants):

All species.

All species except: domestic swine of the family Suidae; American bison, and domestic cattle, sheep and goats of the family Bovidae; races of big-horned sheep (Ovis canadensis) now or formerly indigenous to this state.

(h) Class Gastropoda (slugs, snails, clams)

All species of slugs.

All species of land snails.

In Massachusetts it is illegal to keep a mule on the second floor of a building not in a city unless there are two exits.

Chapter 272 Section 86 (MGL)

It is illegal to frighten a pigeon in Massachusetts.

Chapter 266 Section 132 (MGL) Pigeons; killing or frightening

 Whoever willfully kills pigeons upon, or frightens them from, beds which have been made for the purpose of taking them in nets, by any method, within one hundred rods of the same, except on land lawfully occupied by himself, shall be punished by imprisonment for not more than one month or by a fine of not more than twenty dollars, and shall also be liable for the actual damages to the owner or occupant of such beds.

In the Jupiter Colony Inlet, Florida, you may not launch missiles at birds.

Section 3-1 Bird sanctuary declared

(a) It is hereby declared that all territory embraced within the corporate limits of the municipality shall be a bird sanctuary.

(b) It shall be unlawful for any person within the municipality to shoot, trap or in any manner kill, wound or main any bird of any kind, or at any time to throw at any birds of any kind any missile with slingshots or any other weapon, or to disturb their eggs or their young or their nests.

(Ord. No. 8-59, §§1, 2, 8-10-59)

We've never managed to actually hit a bird with a rock. But give a kid a missile . . .

It is illegal to annoy a bird in any park in the city of Honolulu, Hawaii.

Section 10-1.2

Within the limits of any public park, it is unlawful to annoy any bird.

In Kentucky reptiles cannot be used in conjunction with any church service.

Section 437.060 (KRS)

Any person who displays, handles or uses any kind of reptile in connection with any religious service or gathering shall be fined not less than fifty dollars ($50) nor more than one hundred dollars ($100).

(Passed 1942, from Ky. Stat. sec. 1267a-1.)

All bees entering Kentucky used to need a certificate of health.

Section 252.130 (KRS)

All bees entering Kentucky shall be accompanied by certificates of health, stating that the apiary from which the bees came was free from contagious or infectious disease.

(Passed in 1922; Repealed in 1948)

Have you noticed how many sick bees are out there now?

In Texas a $25 a year license is required to possess a dead alligator.

Chapter 65.00. In this chapter "Alligator" means a living or dead American alligator *(Alligator mississippiensis)*. 65.006. License Required:

(a) No person may take, attempt to take, or possess an alligator in this state unless the person has acquired and possesses an alligator hunter's license. 65.007. License Fees The fees for the licenses issued under this chapter are in the following amounts or in amounts set by the commission, whichever amounts are more: (1) $25 for a resident (Added by Acts 1981, 67th Leg., p. 437, ch. 184, §1, eff. Aug. 31, 1981. Amended by Acts 1985, 69th Leg., ch. 267, art. 2, §59, eff. Sept. 1, 1985.)

In Illinois no one may hunt bullfrogs with a firearm.

Section 5/10-60 Taking of turtles or bullfrogs; illegal devices (515 ILCS)

No person shall take turtles or bullfrogs by commercial fishing devices, including hoop nets, traps, or seines, or by the use of firearms, airguns, or gas guns.

(P.A. 87-833.)

In Massachusetts it is illegal
to drive Texan, Mexican,
Cherokee, or Indian cattle
on a public road.

**Chapter 129 Section 35
(MGL)**

There is no specification

regarding the kinds of

cattle that *can* be

driven down

public roads.

In Massachusetts it is illegal to sell fewer than twenty-four ducklings at a time before May 1, or to sell rabbits, chicks, or ducklings that have been painted a different color.

Chapter 272 Section 80D (MGL)

In Ohio, owners of tigers have one hour to notify officials if their tiger escapes.

Section 2927.21

(A) The owner or keeper of any member of a species of the animal kingdom that escapes from his custody or control and that is not indigenous to this state or presents a risk of serious physical harm to persons or property, or both, shall, within one hour after he discovers or reasonably should have discovered the escape, report it to:

(1) A law enforcement officer of the municipal corporation or township and the sheriff of the county where the escape occurred; and

(2) The clerk of the municipal legislative authority or the township clerk of the township where the escape occurred.

(General Assembly: 116. Bill Number: House Bill 32. Effective Date: 09/11/85)

In Tennessee there is no liability for killing a "proud bitch" running at large.

Section 44-8-411   No liability for killing proud bitch at large.

Any person crippling, killing, or in any way destroying a proud bitch that is running at large shall not be held liable for the damages due to such killing or destruction.

(Acts 1901, ch. 22, §2; Shan., §2853a2; mod. Code 1932, §5084; T.C.A.(orig. ed.), §§44-1411, 44-8-111.)

In Tennessee it is illegal to hunt birds from an airplane.

Section 70-4-109 Hunting from aircraft, watercraft or motor vehicles unlawful

(a) It is unlawful to chase, hunt or kill any wild birds, wild animals or wild fowl in the state of Tennessee from any craft propelled by electric, gasoline, steam or sail power, or airplane or hydroplane or from any automobile or motor vehicle.

(TC. Acts 1951, ch. 115, §36 (Williams, §5178.65); 1979, ch. 237, §1; T.C.A. (orig. ed.), §51-416; Acts 1989, ch. 591, §113)

Using the name or image of Woodsy Owl and Smokey Bear is illegal in the United States.

Title 16 Section 580p-4

(a) Whoever, except as provided by rules and regulations issued by the Secretary, manufactures, uses, or reproduces the character "Smokey Bear," or the name "Smokey Bear," or a facsimile or simulation of such character or name in such a manner as suggests "Smokey Bear" may be enjoined from such manufacture, use, or reproduction at the suit of the Attorney General upon complaint by the Secretary.

(b) Whoever, except as provided by rules and regulations issued by the Secretary, manufactures, uses, or reproduces the character "Woodsy Owl," the name "Woodsy Owl," or the slogan "Give a Hoot, Don't Pollute," or a facsimile or simulation of such character, name, or slogan in such a manner as suggests "Woodsy Owl" may be enjoined from such manufacture, use, or reproduction at the suit of the Attorney General upon complaint by the Secretary.

Things

By Alaskan law, the entire state rarely has emergencies.

Section 44.62.270 State policy.

It is the state policy that emergencies are held to a minimum and are rarely found to exist.

In Oklahoma, hamburgers purchased on Sunday can only be eaten in the restaurant.

21 OS Paragraph 908 (OSCN 2001)

 The following are the acts forbidden to be done on the first day of the week, the doing of any of which is Sabbath-breaking:

4. All manner of public selling, or offering or exposing for sale publicly, of any commodities, except that meats, bread, fish, and all other foods may be sold at any time, and except that food and drink may be sold to be eaten and drank upon the premises where sold, and drugs, medicines, milk, ice, and surgical appliances and burial appliances and all other necessities may be sold at any time of the day.

(R.L. 1910, §2405. Amended by Laws 1913, c. 204, p. 456, §1; Laws 1949, p. 204, §1; Laws 1983, c. 11, §36, emerg. eff. March 22, 1983; Laws 1996, c. 191, §1, emerg. eff. May 16, 1996.)

Kites may not be flown in the village of Schaumburg, Illinois.

Paragraph 132.10 Dangerous Sports

No person shall, at any place in the village, fly kites, play ball or engage in any sport or exercise likely to impede the passage of vehicles and otherwise injure persons, or property or obstruct the business of other persons.

(Ord. 97, passed 5-3-60; Penalty, see §10.99)

Arkansas must be pronounced Ar-kan-SAW

Section 1-4-105   It ain't Kansas

Be it therefore resolved by both houses of the General Assembly, that the only true pronunciation of the name of the state, in the opinion of this body, is that received by the French from the native Indians and committed to writing in the French word representing the sound. It should be pronounced in three (3) syllables, with the final "s" silent, the "a" in each syllable with the Italian sound, and the accent on the first and last syllables. The pronunciation with the accent on the second syllable with the sound of "a" in "man" and the sounding of the terminal "s" is an innovation to be discouraged.

(Concurrent Resolution No. 4, Acts 1881, p. 216; C. & M. Dig., §9181a; Pope's Dig., §11867; A.S.A. 1947, §5-102.)

In Delaware it is illegal to sell perfume as a drink.

Paragraph 901 (DL) Offenses carrying penalty of imprisonment for 3 to 6 months

 (6) Sells, offers for sale, or keeps with the intent to sell for beverage purposes, denatured alcohol, perfume, lotion, tincture, fluid extract or essence, or other liquid or solid not originally manufactured or intended for use as a beverage, containing more than one half of 1 percent of ethyl alcohol by volume, shall, in addition to the payment of costs, be imprisoned not less than 3 nor more than 6 months. Justices of the peace shall have original jurisdiction to hear, try, and finally determine alleged violations of this section.

(38 Del. Laws, c. 18, §§44, 45; Code 1935, §§6172, 6173; 41 Del. Laws, c. 250, §1; 4 Del. C. 1953, §901; 58 Del. Laws, c. 239, §43; 67 Del. Laws, c. 109, §27; 72 Del. Laws, c. 486, §10.)

Moreover, in Delaware it is illegal to sell alcohol where it is illegal.

Paragraph 104 (DL) Sale or shipment out of State

(a) No sale of alcoholic liquor shall be made to a person in a state or a division of a state where such sale is prohibited by law.

(38 Del. Laws, c. 18, §2; Code 1935, §6131(3), (4); 4 Del. C. 1953, §104.)

It is illegal to Reproach Jesus Christ or the Holy Ghost in Massachusetts.

Chapter 272 Section 36 (MGL)

Even if they

misbehave?

Operating a burglar alarm requires police approval in Pinecrest, Florida.

Section 12-23

(a) All persons must complete and submit to the village an emergency contact registration form for their alarm if they operate or cause to be operated an alarm system in the village. A separate registration is required for each alarm system. Upon receipt of a completed registration form, the police department shall issue a numbered alarm sticker to the applicant to facilitate retrieval of registration information.

(Ord. No. 97-17, Paragraph 1, 10-14-97)

In Salt Lake City, Utah, a person can be imprisoned for one month for not returning a library book.

Chapter 10.48.010

Injuring, destroying or failing to return library books prohibited.

B. It is unlawful for any person to fail to return any book, pamphlet or other property of the Free Public Library within five days after the receipt of a notice from the librarian thereof, demanding the return to the library of such property. Any person violating any provision of this chapter is guilty of a misdemeanor and upon conviction thereof shall be punished by a fine of one hundred dollars, or by imprisonment in the county jail not to exceed one month, or both such fine and imprisonment.

(Prior codes §16-11-1 §16-11-2)

It is illegal to sell artificially colored potatoes in Alabama.

Chapter 20-1-30

Sale, offer for sale, etc., of certain artificially colored potatoes. (b) Offense. It shall be unlawful for any individual, partnership, corporation or association to sell, offer for sale or keep for sale in the State of Alabama any artificially colored potatoes; provided, however, that the application of nontoxic coating materials to potatoes when such use does not conceal damage or inferiority is not a violation of this subsection where such polishing or coating material does not contain any coloring agents. The term "artificially colored" as used in this subsection means the application of any natural or synthetic substance to potatoes which changes their natural appearance.

(Acts 1963, No. 534, p. 1146.)

While all U.S. federal employees have a right to a forty-hour work week, no recording clocks may be used to keep track of this time.

Chapter 61—Hours of Work, Subchapter I, General Provisions Section 6106

A recording clock may not be used to record time of an employee of an Executive department in the District of Columbia, except that the Bureau of Engraving and Printing may use such recording clocks.

It is illegal to obstruct any traveled wagon road in Florida for more than two hours.

Section 861.07 Obstructing wagon roads

Whenever any tie cutter or log cutter cutting ties for a railroad or logs for milling purposes shall cut or fell any tree into or across any traveled road, whether it be a county road, a road regularly used by the public, or a neighborhood road, and shall fail to remove the same within 2 hours thereafter so as to free the road from all obstruction therefrom, such tie cutter or log cutter shall be guilty of a misdemeanor of the second degree, punishable as provided in s. 775.082 or s. 775.083, and such person and the person's employer shall be liable or responsible for any and all damages resulting from so obstructing a traveled road.

Flea markets must be one acre or bigger in Columbus, Georgia.

Part II Code of Ordinances, Section 11B-41

 The minimum size of a flea market shall be one acre.

(Ord. No. 87-159, §401, 11-17-87)

One must not ride a bike in Miami, Florida, with a whistle or siren.

Section 8-3 Bell or other warning device

No person shall operate a bicycle unless it is equipped with a bell or device capable of giving a signal audible for a distance of at least 100 feet, but no bicycle shall be equipped with, nor shall any person use upon a bicycle, any siren or whistle.

(Code 1967, §8-3; Code 1980, §8-3)

In Kennesaw, Georgia, every head of household is required to own a firearm.

Part II Code of Ordinances, Section 34-1 Heads of households to maintain firearms

In order to provide for the emergency management of the city, and further in order to provide for and protect the safety, security and general welfare of the city and its inhabitants, every head of household residing in the city limits is required to maintain a firearm, together with ammunition therefor.

(Code 1986, §4-3-10)

GEORGIA

In Duluth, Georgia, it is illegal to litter on one's own property.

Section 10-2 Littering

No person shall throw or dispose of trash, refuse, garbage or waste of any kind or description, or allow the same to be done upon any property, roadways, sidewalks, streets, service areas, public or private property located in the city. This section shall include but not be limited to property owned by or under the control of any such person.

(Ord. of 9-24-70(4), §19)

It is illegal to tie an alligator to a fire hydrant in Michigan.

Section 56-2-7
Obstruction, etc., of fire hydrants

No person shall open any fire hydrant or use any water from the same without first obtaining a permit from the board of fire commissioners. No person shall in any manner obstruct the use of any fire hydrant in the city or have, place or allow to be placed any material or thing in front thereof or connect or tie thereto any object, animal or thing. Any material found as an obstruction, as aforesaid, may be removed by the officers and employees of the board of fire commissioners or the water and sewerage department, at the risk, cost and expense of the owner or claimants.

Rumor held that this law came from New Orleans, but our research led us to the snowy streets of Michigan. We regret that we did not find any specific mention of alligators. We still like our book title.

In Texas maintaining a boat that has sunk is not allowed.

Section 12.28.020 Unlawful activity declared

 In order to protect the boating public and citizens of the city and to protect the public safety and general welfare within the city, it is unlawful for any boat owner, land owner, waterfront lessee or easement owner to maintain or allow a sunken boat, ship or vessel within the city.

(Ord. 3-91 §1 (part))

In Alabama it is illegal to sit in the back seat with your head in the driver's line of sight from the rearview mirror.

Chapter 32-5A-53. Obstruction to driver's view or driving mechanism

(a) No person shall drive a vehicle when it is loaded, or when there are in the front seat such a number of persons as to obstruct the view of the driver to the front or sides of the vehicle or as to interfere with the driver's control over the driving mechanism of the vehicle. (b) No passenger in a vehicle shall ride in such position as to interfere with the driver's view ahead or to the sides, or to interfere with his control over the driving mechanism of the vehicle.

(Acts 1980, No. 80-434, p. 604, §11-104.)

Persons may not use pogo sticks on a city bus in Fairfax County, Virginia.

Section 85-1-3. Conduct on public vehicle regulated

(a) It shall be unlawful for passengers or occupants, while aboard a public passenger vehicle not used primarily for the transportation of schoolchildren while said public passenger vehicle is transporting passengers in regular route service, contract service, special or community-type service, or any person in a rail transit station to:

(9) Wear, operate, utilize or cause to be operated or utilized roller skates, skateboards, pogo sticks, noncollapsible baby carriages, wagons or cars unless so directed by an employee or agent of the operator;

(16-75-17, 5-12-75; Va. Code Ann., § 56-329; 22-77-85; 14-84-85; 19-85-85.)

In Schaumburg, Illinois, no poison may be sold unless it is to be used with "proper motives."

Paragraph 130.05

No poisonous medicine, decoction or substance shall be held for sale or sold, except for lawful purposes and with proper motives, and by persons competent to give the proper directions and precautions as to the use of the same. No bottle, box, parcel or receptacle thereof shall be delivered to any person unless the same is marked "poison" nor to any person whom the party delivering the same has reason to think intends it for any illegal or improper use or purpose.

(Ord. 97, passed 5-3-60); Penalty, see §10.99)

It is a crime to forget to close a gate in Nevada.

Section 207.220 (NRS) Penalty for not closing gates

 1. Any person or persons opening and passing through gates or bars when gates or bars are placed in fences enclosing fields, or in fences partly enclosing lands, and not shutting and fastening the same, shall be deemed guilty of a misdemeanor.

2. The provisions of this section shall not apply to gates in towns and cities nor gates necessary in the approach to any building or works where the passing through or into fields or lands is not contemplated.

[1911 C&P §504; RL §6769; NCL §10451]

No one may park under a bridge in New Jersey.

Permanent Statutes Section 27:19-6 Bridges and viaducts to connect highways 39:4-138

Except when necessary to avoid conflict with other traffic or in compliance with the directions of a traffic or police officer or traffic sign or signal, no operator of a vehicle shall stand or park the vehicle in any of the following places:

11. Upon any bridge or other elevated structure upon a highway, or within a highway tunnel or underpass, or on the immediate approaches thereto except where space for parking is provided.

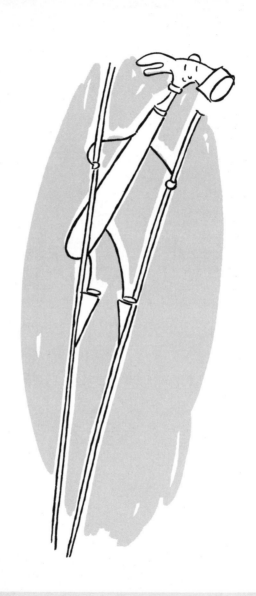

In Massachusetts it is illegal to wear stilts while working on a construction site.

Chapter 149 Section 129B (MGL)

Whoever, being engaged in construction work, requires or knowingly permits any person employed by him in such work to use certain devices, commonly called stilts, designed to be attached to the feet or legs of such employee for the purpose of elevating him to high placed or positioned work, shall be punished.

Boobie traps are illegal in Moab, Utah.

Chapter 9.32.040 Traps and deadfalls

 No person shall arrange any trap, prepare any deadfall or dig any pit to injure another's person or property.

(Prior code §17-43)

Ice from outside El Paso, Texas, may not be distributed there.

Section 10.24.010 Ice manufactured outside city

It is unlawful to sell, offer for sale, or distribute in the city any ice manufactured outside the city, except ice manufactured wholly from distilled water.

(Prior code §15-7.1)

In Biloxi, Mississippi, the ice cream man may not use his speaker to attract customers.

Section 11-1-4

 The following acts, among others, are declared to be loud or disturbing noises in violation of sections 11-1-2 through 11-1-4, but such enumeration shall not be deemed to be exclusive, namely:

(3) Use of loudspeakers, amplifiers for advertising. The using, operating or permitting to be played, used or operated of any radio receiving set, musical instrument, loudspeaker, sound amplifier or other machine or device for the producing or reproducing of sound which is cast upon the public streets for the purpose of commercial advertising or attracting the attention of the public to any building or structure.

Coasting one's car downhill in neutral is illegal in Rhode Island.

Title 31 Motor and Other vehicles Paragraph 31-22-6 Coasting prohibited

(a) The driver of any motor vehicle when traveling upon a down grade shall not coast with the gears of the vehicle in neutral.

(b) The driver of a commercial motor vehicle, when traveling upon a down grade, shall not coast with the clutch disengaged.

It is illegal to injure a football goalpost in Massachusetts.

Chapter 266 Section 104A (MGL) Goalposts; penalty for destruction

Whoever willfully and without right destroys, injures or removes a goalpost on a football field shall be punished by a fine of not less than fifty nor more than two hundred dollars.

In Cambridge, Massachusetts, one may not throw orange peels on the sidewalk.

Section 12.16.100

It is illegal to shake carpets in the street, or to throw orange peels on the sidewalk.

In La Plata, Maryland, it is illegal to operate a taxi with three doors.

Section 176-14 Cleanliness and sanitation; number of doors required

B. It shall be unlawful to operate any taxicab which has fewer than four (4) doors.

In Minot, North Dakota, a car can only be considered a visual nuisance if it is unregistered.

Section 22-1

(a) In addition to such other items or conditions which may be declared to be a nuisance under other chapters of this Code of Ordinances, the following items or conditions designated hereafter are declared to be nuisances:

Similar laws apply in Florida and Vicksburg, Mississippi.

(2) Visual nuisances: An accumulation or pile of unsightly materials which constitute an eyesore, such as, by way of illustration and not of limitation, the following: a. Junked, abandoned, disassembled, inoperative or unregistered automobiles (excluding, however, automobiles which are currently licensed, registered, and operable:

In Oregon it is illegal to pump your own gas unless you own the dispensing device and are properly trained.

Section 480.330 Operation of gasoline dispensing device by public prohibited

No owner, operator or employee of any filling station, service station, garage or other dispensary where Class 1 flammable liquids are dispensed at retail, shall permit any person other than the owner, operator or employee to use or manipulate any pump, hose, pipe or other device for dispensing such liquids into the fuel tank of a motor vehicle or other retail container.

Luckily we have "gas dispensing technicians" to do this important work for us in Oregon— and New Jersey.

In South Carolina only fruit may be sold by itinerants within a half mile of a church.

Title 40—Professions and Occupations Section 40-41-70 Sales prohibited within one-half mile of religious camp ground

It shall be unlawful for any itinerant trader or tradesman, other than an established dealer of the community, to offer for sale any goods, wares or merchandise within one half of a mile of any camp ground or other place of religious meeting, while meetings are in progress, outside any incorporated town or city, except with the permission of the trustees or other board of management of such meeting. But this section shall not apply to vendors of fresh fruit or vegetables or any farm product. Any person violating the provisions of this section shall be guilty of a misdemeanor and, upon conviction, shall be fined in a sum not exceeding fifty dollars or be imprisoned not exceeding twenty days.

145

In Rhode Island it is illegal to place a windmill within twenty-five rods of any traveled road.

TITLE 11—Criminal Offenses Paragraph 11-22-5 Penalty for unlawful windmill

A rod is 5 yards, 6 inches.

Every person who shall erect, locate or run any windmill within twenty-five (25) rods of any traveled street or road shall be fined for every offense not exceeding five hundred dollars ($500) nor less than one hundred dollars ($100), one-half (1/2) inuring to the use of the town where the offense shall have been committed and one-half (1/2) to the use of the state.

In Texas hoes are required to have handles at least four feet in length.

Paragraph 52.021 Minimum Length of Hoe Handles

 (a) An employer of agricultural laborers may not require an employee to use a hoe that has a handle shorter than four feet while performing agricultural labor in a commercial farming operation.

(Acts 1993, 73rd Leg., ch. 269, §1, eff. Sept. 1, 1993.)

It is illegal to drive a vehicle as an advertisement in Madison, Wisconsin.

Chapter 12 Vehicle Code Section 12.128
Miscellaneous restrictions on parking

(2) Advertising Display. No person shall drive or park a vehicle on any highway for the primary purpose of displaying advertising; provided, however, that this ordinance shall not be deemed to prohibit a street parade sponsored by business, industrial or trade organizations for the purpose of promoting a general business theme or program where no advertising matter relating to a particular make or brand of article or product or a particular business outlet is displayed.

In Massachusetts defacing a milk carton is punishable by a ten-dollar fine.

Chapter 266 Section 128 (MGL)
Milk cans; defacement

Whoever, without the consent of the owner thereof, knowingly and willfully effaces, alters or covers over, or procures to be effaced, altered or covered over, the name, initial or device of any dealer in milk, marked or stamped upon a milk can, or whoever, with intent to defraud and without such consent, detains or uses in his business any such can having the name, initial or device of any dealer in milk so marked or stamped thereon, shall be punished by a fine of not more than ten dollars.

In Texas windshield wipers are required, even though a windshield is not.

Paragraph 547.603
Windshield Wipers Required

A motor vehicle shall be equipped with a device that is operated or controlled by the operator of the vehicle and that cleans moisture from the windshield. The device shall be maintained in good working condition.

(Acts 1995, 74th Leg., ch. 165, §1, eff. Sept. 1, 1995.)

No law exists requiring vehicles to have a windshield; in fact, several laws refer specifically to vehicles without a windshield.

It is illegal to keep a car dealership open on a Sunday in Wisconsin.

Section 218.0116 (1)(k) (WSL)

Nothing in this paragraph shall apply to any person who conscientiously believes that the 7th day of the week from sunset Friday to sunset Saturday should be observed as the Sabbath.

You may not affix the U.S. flag to a bar of soap that is for sale.

TITLE 4—Flag and Seal, Seat of Government, and the States, Chapter 1, Section 3

Any person who, within the District of Columbia, in any manner, for exhibition or display, shall place or cause to be placed any word, figure, mark, picture, design, drawing, or any advertisement of any nature upon any flag, standard, colors, or ensign of the United States of America; or shall expose or cause to be exposed to public view any such flag, standard, colors, or ensign upon which shall have been printed, painted, or otherwise placed, or to which shall be attached, appended, affixed, or annexed any word, figure, mark, picture, design, or drawing, or any advertisement of any nature; or who, within the District of Columbia, shall manufacture, sell, expose for sale, or to public view, or give away or have in possession for sale, or to be given away or for use for any purpose, any article or substance being an article of merchandise, or a receptacle for merchandise or article or thing for carrying or transporting merchandise, upon which shall have been printed, painted, attached, or otherwise placed a representation of any such flag, standard, colors, or ensign, to advertise, call attention to, decorate, mark, or distinguish the article or substance on which so placed shall be deemed guilty of a misdemeanor and shall be punished by a fine not exceeding $100 or by imprisonment for not more than thirty days, or both, in the discretion of the court.

Acknowledgments

We would like to thank our friends who worked to make Dumblaws.com a success. David Bentsen, Grant Kersey, Antonio Haynes, and Paddy Ferriter all helped make our site happen.

We would also like to thank our editor, Stephen Morrow, and our illustrator, Ward Schumacher, for making this book possible.

Finally, we both would like to express our love and gratitude to our parents for their continued support, as well as our many thanks to Frank Futyma who showed us the potential of our work and guided us as our little business faced new challenges.